wisdom from a
HUMBLE JELLYFISH

wisdom *from a*
HUMBLE
JELLYFISH

And Other Self-Care Rituals
from Nature

RANI SHAH

illustrations by
GEMMA CORRELL

DEY ST.

An Imprint of WILLIAM MORROW

HarperCollins books may be purchased for educational, business,
or sales promotional use. For information, please email the Special
Markets Department at SPsales@harpercollins.com.

FIRST EDITION

DESIGNED BY RENATA DE OLIVEIRA

Spider web and wave illustrations by Om Yos, Ptaha I / Shutterstock, Inc.
Earth illustration by Bibadash / Shutterstock, Inc.

Library of Congress Cataloging-in-Publication Data
has been applied for.

ISBN 978-0-06-293173-3

20 21 22 23 24   WOR   10 9 8 7 6 5 4 3 2 1

FOR ALL MY WISE JELLYFISH:

My parents and brother,
Kinnari, Sanjeev, and Rohan
My grandparents,
Vasanti, Vimla, Surendra,
and Hasmukh
My favorite, Utsav

I am so glad that teaching me
how to read turned out to be useful.

CONTENTS

INTRODUCTION:

WELCOME TO THE JUNGLE

Today is a wonderful day! It's the day you woke up and thought to yourself, "Man, I wish I knew what an axolotl was and what it could teach me about self-care." If this *was* the first thing that popped into your head today, then yes, I *am* a powerful psychic. But if not, and you've never heard of an axolotl, don't sweat it. I'm here to teach you all about how this adorable little creature and an array of other plant and animal friends can improve your life. Hang on tight! You're in for quite the adventure.

Hiking, safari, deep-sea diving, casually walking on the moon—the numerous ways that humans have come up with for exploring our planet and interacting with her inhabitants are mind-bogglingly impressive. But exploring the natural world isn't reserved for the adventurous and wealthy. Exploration is meant for anyone who is curious. The notably curious of history have included the famous Greek philosopher Thales,[*] who by observing the stars successfully predicted the timing of the first solar eclipse, and my personal favorite, household name Charles Darwin, who developed our modern theory of evolution by studying animals on the Galápagos Islands. As a non-notable person who is curious about nature, I once tried to mimic bird calls to elicit a reaction from the local flock, but only succeeded in scaring away small children.

Our humble abode, planet earth, is an astonishing thing. For four and a half billion years, the planet has been creating intricate communities known as "ecosystems," each consisting of thousands, if not millions, of different plants and animals. And each of these plants and animals has evolved its own unique set of traits and behaviors in order to live, thrive, and reproduce. Whether we're talking about a flower using its brightly colored petals to attract insects for pollination or a cat using its fantastic night vision to capture prey in low light, plants and animals are able to exist and thrive only if they have adapted traits and behaviors that prioritize their well-being.

How does this relate to self-care? Defined by the *Oxford English Dictionary* as the "practice of taking an active role in protecting one's own well-being and happiness," self-care is

---

[*] *Thales is known as the grandfather of naturalism, a philosophical movement defined as the idea or belief that only natural (as opposed to supernatural or spiritual) laws and forces operate in the world.*

something that creatures in the wild have been putting into practice since the very beginning. For plants and animals in the wild, self-care, in its most basic sense, begins with avoiding predators and successfully sourcing food to stay alive. These guys are regularly faced with pressing questions like "Will I get killed today?" and "Will I eat today?" So the meaning of "thrive" is very different for a creature in the wild than it is for us modern humans.

Most of us aren't hunting or cultivating our own food, let alone fleeing from predators. For humans, seemingly nothing should stand in the way of our well-being. And yet so many of us are plagued by anxiety, stress, and unhappiness. While we may not be worried about physical predators lurking in the bush waiting to eat us, the lives we lead and the environments we live in *do* cause us stress. Take modern technology, for example. Although technology has led to many advances that benefit our health, significant negative health effects are also associated with our attachment to our computers and smartphones. Many of us are socially isolated behind our screens, where we are also more sedentary than at any other time in human history, and we work long hours and face high levels of stress in our workplaces. The United States is one of the most overworked countries in the world. According to a study in the medical journal *The Lancet*, American workers, compared with workers in other countries, including those in East Asia and across Europe, are not only among the most stressed but also at a significantly higher risk of developing heart disease.

*Self-care:
the practice
of taking action
to preserve
or improve one's
own health.*

So our obsession with social media and our jobs may be killing us. Fun. Is there anything we can do about it? Before you panic, let's take a closer look at modern understandings of self-care, which do not require avoiding technology completely or going off to live on a mountaintop. The reality is that unless you've hit the Megamillions jackpot or got into Bitcoin as an early adopter, you have to go to work—where you eventually need to interact with a smartphone or a computer in some form. Self-care, in the modern sense, is all about balance. It involves more than throwing on a face mask or inhaling some essential oils. In a broader sense, self-care is about prioritizing your mental, physical, and emotional well-being—whether that means getting more sleep, exercising regularly, or dressing up and feeling fancy for no reason.

Self-care is ultimately about making sure you remember to always be kind to yourself.

Though suddenly trendy, self-care is an age-old concept. Eastern medicine has embraced it for centuries, taking a preventative approach to mental and physical health rather than just treating disease. From social media influencers promoting the latest wellness fads to expensive retail therapy being branded as "self-care," we hear this term thrown around a lot and misused, and this can be confusing. Spending tons of money or avoiding social engagements is *not* what self-care is about. Truly understanding what self-care consists of can help us shake off any hesitations we might have when it comes to putting ourselves first and devoting time to our goals without feeling guilty. Self-care is not selfish—it's about progressing toward a better version of ourselves, both mentally and physically, so that we can achieve our long-term goals, nurture important relationships, and live life to its fullest potential.

To survive and thrive through multiple generations, all living organisms must possess one essential trait: the ability to properly care for themselves. In the wild, self-care can be particularly dramatic and colorful. For instance:

- OCTOPUSES* have evolved to camouflage underwater to escape predators and capture prey.

- TURTLES have evolved a tough shell to compensate for being such a slow and easy target for predators.

- CHEETAHS have evolved to become predators of ungodly speed.

Life only flourishes when creatures of all shapes and sizes can successfully engage in self-care. For us humans, the stresses of modern life can make our defense systems feel paper-thin. It's time to get back to the basics and look to the animals and plants in the wonderfully wild world around us for some valuable lessons on how to combat stress, anxiety, and potential burnout.

So strap on those backpacks, hydrate, and prepare to be led on a safari of self-care! From the energy-efficient tranquility of the jellyfish to the blinding (and deafening) beauty of the mantis shrimp to the resilience of the porcupine, we can learn

---

*Yes, "octopuses" is the correct plural term. We'll get back to this later in the book. Stop freaking out.

so much from earth's delightful critters about living harmoniously and taking better care of ourselves. And I hope that you will also be inspired to give these creatures a little extra love in return, by respecting and protecting the beautiful planet that we all share. Because caring for nature is self-care for us all.

wisdom from a
HUMBLE JELLYFISH

THE
PORCUPINE

Fun fact: a baby porcupine is, appropriately, called a "porcupette."

Setbacks can seriously hurt. A bad breakup, a negative review at work, getting laid off, losing your home—these things are painful.

What if your setback was impaling yourself with a quill? Ouch. Literally painful. For our prickly pal the porcupine, it's a real problem. Porcupines spend a good deal of their time up in trees, and as we all know, what goes up must come down. When the porcupine finally decides to come down from the tree, she has to make her way backward, with her behind facing the ground. Since porcupines have no exact way of knowing when they're near the ground, they will often let go prematurely and fall the rest of the way, impaling themselves with their quills.

Sound gruesome? Don't get sad just yet, because the North American tree porcupine has cleverly evolved to survive fatal infections, like tetanus or gangrene, that can result from impaling themselves. Coated in fatty acids that prevent bacterial growth, the porcupine's unique quills possess antibacterial, penicillin-like properties that eliminate their risk of deadly infection. Porcupines have their own biological system in place to accommodate painful injuries. Bouncing back from a potentially life-threatening setback is literally in their DNA.

For us humans, recovering from everyday setbacks may not be ingrained in our DNA, but a shift in mind-set can help us prepare for the many challenges that we encounter. Channel the (somewhat prickly) resilience of the porcupine and embrace these principles for dealing with difficult setbacks:

"IF YOU'VE NEVER FAILED, YOU'VE NEVER TRIED ANYTHING NEW": This quote from Albert Einstein perfectly captures what it means to try anything worthwhile. When you set out to achieve a new goal, failure is almost always inevitable, but it isn't indicative of your potential. It's a temporary setback showing you that you don't always have control over your situation. Keep at it!

DON'T LET FAILURE SURPRISE YOU: Anticipating failure doesn't mean that you're setting the bar low. It's just a way to better prepare for the unexpected— like impaling yourself with your own quill. A brilliant friend of mine introduced me to what I like to call the "apply to fail" tactic. As a writer, she frequently submits her writing to magazines and journals, and that process involves a lot of vulnerability, time, and rejection. To cope with rejection and also to increase her chances of success, she expects ten rejections for every "yes" that she gets. Sound harsh? Try it and you'll see that the first rejection is always the hardest, but after that every "no" is just part of the quota. And when you get a "yes," it's that much more satisfying.

PICK YOURSELF UP AGAIN, AND AGAIN: US Army officer and cavalry commander George Custer once said, "It's not how many times you get knocked down that count, it's how many times you get back

"It's not how many times you get knocked down that count, it's how many times you get back up."

—GEORGE CUSTER,
US Army office and cavalry commander

up." From major scientific breakthroughs to learning to ride a bike, we have to make multiple attempts before we can find and bask in our success. But why do some setbacks really knock us down hard? It often has to do with the number of times we try. If you've had your heart broken more than once, you probably handled your first heartbreak very differently from a later one. Focusing on your next course of action after a setback is the best way to bounce back. What's a practical way to do this? Make a good old-fashioned to-do list. However, instead of listing your next steps after a major letdown, such as being fired from a job, create a list from the perspective of someone else. Imagine that your friend is the one who's been fired and you are giving him advice. This will allow you to get out of your own head and distance yourself from the situation, so you can make a levelheaded choice about what to do next. Sometimes it's easier to get out of our own head by pretending it's someone else's.

Take it from the hardy porcupine:
*You can't control whether or not you get hurt.
It's inevitable that you will get hurt at some point. But you
can control how much you allow it to affect you.*

THE
DRAGONFLY

*A finely calibrated killing
machine with a 95 percent
success rate in capturing its prey
roams the earth with us.*

But don't board up your home and hide the dog just yet. Fortunately, the dragonfly is only a threat to flies, mosquitoes, gnats, and a handful of some very unlucky butterflies.

Dragonflies have an ability that's unique in the insect world: they are keen enough to predict and intercept their future meal's movements—they can predict the exact path of their target before it even has a chance to fly away. With concentration comparable to that of a human, the dragonfly is one of the planet's most formidable hunters. Typically, predators conduct their hunt by fixating on their prey—once they spot a potential target, they move directly toward it. Also known as "classical pursuit," this type of fixation is akin to reaching for that last cookie: we humans see the cookie and aim for its exact location, without accounting for any sudden movements. If you're accustomed to cookies that move, please reach out to me to explain the life you are living. Dragonflies, in contrast, not only fixate on their prey but also intercept its movement by homing in on its path.

A killer sense of focus is essential to achieving your goals. However, focus isn't always enough. Being prepared for any sudden changes you encounter along the way is vital to accomplishing your objective. For example, when setting a deadline for yourself, add a few extra days to account for the unexpected. Put your phone on Silent to help eliminate the pesky urge to constantly check your phone when you're trying to get work done. Make sure your devices are charged, so you never fall victim to forgetting your charger at home. Plan and focus on your big-picture dreams by writing out your long-term goals in a planner, even if you have to set an arbitrary deadline, such as "finish screenplay by April 15." You may not finish that screenplay by the fifteenth, but at least you will have gotten started, which is one step in the right direction. If you spell out your goals in a tangible way, chances are you'll be more focused than ever on meeting your targets.

Take it from the cunning dragonfly:
make your targets easier to achieve by recalibrating and being the most prepared you can possibly be.

THE
SPIDER

Spiders. No one wants to see one in their home, in the wild, in pictures, or anywhere for that matter.

My very professional ranking of the three best kinds of webs are:

1. The World Wide Web

2. *Charlotte's Web*

3. The bolas spider's sneaky lasso web, which she uses to capture moths

If you're one of the rare people who absolutely adores our eight-legged friends, then you are in for a treat. We're going to learn about (and *from*) the clever spider and its ingenious webs.

But before we get *entangled* in the details, it's important to note what makes spiders (and their webs) so admirable: their versatility. Depending on the region of the world you live in, when you imagine a spider's web, a distinct shape will come to mind. For some, it's the ubiquitous circular shape popular in Halloween decor and spooky movies. For others, especially those in Australia, it may be the less common funnel-shaped web that comes to mind. No matter the species, region, or shape, the primary function of a spiderweb always remains the same: to capture prey.

There are dozens of different types of spiderwebs—such as tangle webs, sheet webs, and funnel webs, to name a few. Here's a deep dive into the webs of three unforgettable spider species.

The Triangle Spider

Commonly known as the triangle spider, spiders of the *Hyptiotes* genus spin a rather untraditional web. True to its name, *Hyptiotes* attaches its web to three separate points, making an isosceles triangle. One of the points of the triangle is *Hyptiotes* herself. As she waits for flies or large moths to get caught in her web, the triangle spider keeps the web taut—so taut that even the wind can barely move it—by holding it be-

If you're hungry, you'll be pleased to know that some people swear that a baked golden silk orb weaver tastes exactly like high-quality pâté.

tween her two front legs, while the rest of her body grasps something sturdy nearby, such as a tree branch.

Once a poor victim flies right into the web, the spider immediately feels the vibrations from the flailing insect. Most spiders walk toward their prey once it's stuck in their web and then wrap them in silk. But not *Hyptiotes*. Instead of moving toward her catch, she swiftly releases the tension point of her web, causing the entire thing to collapse upon the prey, which is immediately entangled in spider silk.

But never fear, at one-sixth of an inch in size, this nonvenomous spider isn't anything for us humans to worry about . . . for now.

The Golden Silk Orb Weaver

The golden silk orb weaver of the genus *Nephila* is found in warmer areas of the world with dense vegetation, such as the southeastern United States, southern Africa, and Australia. *Nephila* spiders are basically an arachnophobe's worst nightmare. Their bright yellow-green legs can be up to two inches long, and there have been reports of *Nephila* species being found in Madagascar that are nearly five inches long—almost the length of a dollar bill. Yes, I am also traumatized.

While these spiders are the ultimate creepy-crawlies, they make up for it with their beautiful gold webs. *Nephila* spiders are the architects of the largest webs found in Australia—they have been known to reach up to three feet in diameter. Pigments in the spider's silk known as carotenoids—the same pigment that gives carrots their signature orange color—cause these golden webs to blend in with their sunny surroundings almost invisibly, reflecting off the sunlight and greenery around them. The brighter the golden strands, the more bees and other insects are drawn to them. Interestingly, the golden silk orb weaver spins less vibrant webs in darker areas of a forest, revealing that this spider is capable of controlling the pigment it releases in its silk depending on where it is constructing a web.

The Bolas Spider

Bolas spiders of the *Mastophora* genus are both masters of disguise and master hunters. Cleverly perched on a leaf, the bolas spider, with its round, speckled red-brown-and-white bottom, has developed the perfect method for warding off predators: it can look exactly like a wad of bird poop. With its predators at bay, the bolas spider can focus on more *delicate* matters. Come evening, she begins by dangling herself from a strand of her own silk. Next, she creates another thin strand with a small, sticky globule at the far end: picture a string tied to a small pebble. (Fun fact: this lassolike strand with a sticky end gave the bolas spider its name: a *bolas* is a rope that has heavy weights attached to the end of it and is used by humans to hunt animals.)

As the bolas spider dangles her deadly silk strands, she doesn't wait for prey to zoom by. She has a much better strategy! She begins by emitting copycat female pheromones of the local moth species to lure male moths toward her. Once an unfortunate moth picks up the scent and begins to

A bolas is a rope that has heavy weights attached to the end of it and is used by humans to hunt animals.

fly closer, the spider's sensory hairs pick up on his general direction of movement, and now she strikes! The bolas spider swings her bolas at the moth, immediately capturing it and sealing its sticky fate. One venomous bite and a bit of swift silk wrapping later, the moth is ready to be served.

Plot twist: The bolas spider's aggressive chemical mimicry is not reserved for capturing a single species of moth. For example, the *M. hutchinsoni*, a species of bolas spider, will emit the pheromones of two separate moth species during two different times at night. The bristly cutworm moth is most active after sunset, which is when the spider emits pheromones to trap it. Later, the smoky tetanolita moth is active mostly after 11:00 P.M., which is when *M. hutchinsoni* begins phasing out the pheromones targeted at the bristly cutworm and switches to attracting her new target.

Bird poop, sticky lasso, and faux moth pheromones—the bolas spider knows exactly how to get what she wants.

Webs. Webs. Webs.

Having roamed the planet for 380 million years, the thousands of different species of spiders have figured out a thing or two about how to make it on earth. The spider's trick to survival? Devising creative methods to reach the target. From the bolas spider throwing a lasso to the triangle spider constructing the absolute opposite of a love triangle, spiders have all evolved to achieve their goals in their own unique way.

Whether your goal is career-related or personal, there's no one, single way to accomplish it. Landing a job interview is no longer as simple as filling out an application. You've got to network, maybe get lucky with an online application, ace the interview, and then negotiate your salary if given an offer. Finding love isn't as straightforward as setting up a profile on a dating app and swiping right. You've got to take the perfect profile pic, wine and dine your potential match, and absolutely avoid anyone with a LIVE, LAUGH, LOVE tattoo. Reaching your financial goals goes beyond swearing off avocado toast forever. You've got to make a budget, save up, invest in your 401(k), make a plan to completely pay off those student loans—ugh! If there was a single, right way to reach our goals, wouldn't we all have it figured out by now?

Take it from the nimble spider:
There are multiple ways to weave a web to achieve your goals.

THE
SUNFLOWER

*It's hard not to perk up
when you come across a buzzy,
yellow sunflower.*

The next time you pass a sunflower field, take note— you'll see that the most mature flowers are facing east.

Seeming to have figured out how to always look on the bright side, this symbol of joy and loyalty with magnificent blooms averages from six to ten feet tall. It is the epitome of beauty *and* brains.

A common misconception is that sunflowers in full bloom move their heads east to west during the day to try to follow the sun. In fact, mature sunflowers don't move with the sun, but young sunflower buds sure do. In their early stages of growth, sunflower buds shift their position to follow the movement of the sun as it moves east to west. This allows them to grab as much sunlight as possible, increasing their growth rates. But how exactly do these buds move? The secret is in their stems. The flexible portion of the sunflower's stem, right below the bud, allows these beauties to always find the sun. The cells on the side of the stem opposite to where the sun is shining can stretch, ensuring that the flower's head is always tilted sunward.

Once the sun dips below the horizon, the sunflower bud prepares for the next day by moving its head to face east, patiently waiting for the next sunrise. The next time you pass a sunflower field, take note—you'll see that the most mature flowers are facing east. As the bud blossoms, it remains in its eastward-facing position, which allows the fully grown flower to absorb as much sunlight as possible at the beginning of each day. Clearly, the sunflower has it figured out when it comes to a ritual for starting and ending its day.

We can learn a lot from the sunflower about looking on the bright side. Thinking like an optimist can increase your life span, improve your relationships, and ultimately lead to an overall healthier life. Being an optimist, of course, is easier said than done. After all, we may even owe our survival as a species to our tendency toward pessimism, which historically has kept us from becoming someone else's lunch or succumbing to deadly plants. However, psychologists have found that practices like looking for a silver lining or displaying gratitude not only increase our life spans but also aid in living a happier, more fulfilled life. So how exactly do you wake up and start looking on the bright side? According to world-renowned psychotherapist Dr. Martin Seligman (also known as "the father of positive psychology"), you can start with two simple exercises:

> SAY THANK YOU: Write a letter of gratitude to a close friend, partner, or family member (assuming that you like them, of course). Then read it out loud to the lucky recipient. Research shows that this practice can boost your mood for almost four weeks! And it works not just for you. Imagine how great you can make your loved ones feel with this quick exercise!

> YOUR THREE GOOD THINGS: Just as the sunflower aligns itself positively at the end of each day, you can do the same. Before you go to bed, recall and jot down three positive things that occurred that day. Next to each item, also jot down

why it happened. For instance, "Got a compliment on my hair today . . . because I've been getting trims more often." This exercise is not intended to falsely inflate your ego, but rather to remind you of all the positive moments in your life!

Take it from the radiant sunflower:
Looking on the bright side of life isn't just a pleasant exercise—it helps you grow stronger.

THE
JELLYFISH

Taking a cue from one of the most energy-efficient animals in the world is never a bad idea.

With ancestors spanning back 500 million years (possibly even 700 million), the jellyfish may very well be three times as old as the first dinosaur species to roam the earth. Besides being responsible for literally stirring the world's oceans, jellyfish have an incredible way of getting around. They propel themselves forward using a distinctive suction method.

If you're not familiar with how jellyfish look when they swim, imagine all of your fingers gently coming together as if you're picking something up, and then releasing it.* To swim forward, jellyfish must contract their bodies and then relax in order to initiate a second wave of motion. Without that crucial step of relaxing their bodies in between strokes, there would be no forward movement in their swimming. This brief break in motion is also what makes the jellyfish one of the most energy-efficient creatures on the planet! Having a watery, low-density, jelly-filled center (called mesoglea) also aids the jellyfish in moving through the oceans with little to no resistance.

As humans, we know that relaxing and giving ourselves mental breaks is important, but how exactly does this relate to the gospel of the jellyfish? Well, your brain is one powerful muscle that is constantly making decisions (upward of 35,000 on average per day) and is constantly stimulated by its environment.† Taking a break when your brain needs to make a decision is similar to the "contraction" period of the jellyfish's body. In fact, if you don't take breaks, you'll be prone to anxiety and burnout, not to mention a general decrease in productivity and focus.

* This is also the secret handshake for all readers of this book. You're welcome!
† Oooh! Shiny object!

Taking a break or indulging in a moment of rest, whether it be going for a walk or cleaning your work space, not only helps clear your mind but also increases your ability to get things done in the immediate future. And take note: jellyfish don't skimp on their breaks—it's a vital part of their process. To do this, try scheduling designated break times to make sure that you are relaxing just as efficiently as you are working. Taking a short walk every 30 to 60 minutes while at work is great for mind and body. If walking isn't an option in the middle of a busy day, try the 20-20-20 rule: every 20 minutes, look at least 20 feet away from your computer screen for about 20 seconds—give those eyes a rest!

Even when taking a well-deserved vacation isn't an option, our minds respond in a positive way when experiencing novelty. Take "better" breaks throughout the course of your day by changing up your typical walking route around the neighborhood, or scheduling in micro-moments that excite you. Whether it's taking the time to pause for your favorite snack or seeing a friend for lunch, creating moments for your body and mind to truly feel at ease is just as important as getting your work done.

Take it from the humble jellyfish:
There is no moving forward without a little relaxation.

THE
VERVET
MONKEY

Vervet monkeys are native to South Africa and are known for what scientists refer to as their "alarm communication structure."

Not unlike humans, these monkeys loudly vocalize with different noises when trying to convey a message, especially when it's life-or-death information like, "Look out, there's a predator!" Vervet monkeys will scream a warning based on the type of predator posing a threat: Snake? "Get in the tree!" Eagle? "Get low and hide in a bush!"

What's particularly interesting, and useful, is the way vervet monkeys take into account adult speech versus juvenile speech. If a juvenile issues a warning, adults will wait until an adult verifies the juvenile's message. Sound judgmental? It's not. Young vervets haven't quite nailed the lingo, and often they'll accidentally switch up their warning signals, which could be fatal for the troop.[*] Imagine listening to a young monkey instructing everyone to retreat to the ground when a snake is present, instead of safely escaping into the trees.

Instead of getting angry at the juvenile, the troop understands that mistakes are a part of the learning process, and the adults make sure to consult with one another before making a decision. This system allows the monkeys to manage mistakes in a sustainable way—something most humans have yet to master.

Think about the last time you made a stressful mistake. Maybe you lost your keys, forgot to pay your rent on time, or even screamed *"Snake!"* on an airplane. Your inner dialogue

---

[*] *A troop is a group of monkeys. They can also be called a barrel or a carload. On second thought, I should have called them a carload. How fun!*

INNER DIALOGUE SAMPLES:

"I'm so stupid."

"This is why everyone is annoyed with me at work."

"I'm such a joke."

during this stressful time might have been harsh, since we all find it easy to mentally berate ourselves for making mistakes.

"I'm so stupid."

"This is why everyone is annoyed with me at work."

"I'm such a joke."

Rough, but we've all probably had similar thoughts after a wrong turn. Although it is completely normal to express anger or frustration over a mishap, the real issue arises if those feelings never seem to properly subside. Dwelling on mistakes prevents us from learning and moving forward.

If adult vervet monkeys did not allow younger monkeys to practice warning the troop, there could be dire consequences down the line. But given leeway by the adults, young vervets develop the skills they need to communicate danger once they reach adulthood.

A simple, yet effective way to reduce the sting of a mistake is to remember one key thing: every mistake is a learning opportunity. And you are not alone! Calling someone the wrong name or even losing your phone feels terrible in the moment. However, you're not the first person in the history of mankind to make that mistake. Vervet monkeys empathize with others when they make a blunder and help them learn from it. Be like a vervet monkey.

Self-care is all about being kind to yourself. Forgiving mistakes in others is much easier when you don't judge yourself harshly for making mistakes yourself. So next time you or a colleague flubs a presentation or accidentally hits Reply All (again), pull your empathy card out and keep an open mind to the lessons that can be learned.

Take it from the savvy vervet:
Mistakes happen. Rather than letting your missteps define you, allow them to teach you.

THE
AXOLOTL

Introducing . . . what is quite possibly the friendliest-looking amphibian in the entire animal kingdom, the axolotl (pronounced ACK-suh-LAH-tuhl).

Scientists have yet to find a limit on how often a single axolotl can regrow the same part of its body.

Named by the Aztecs after the god of lightning and death, Xolotl, axolotl translates to "water monster"—though in reality the axolotl is more of a "water teddy bear." Today the axolotl dwells in the waters surrounding Mexico City, not too far from where the ancient Aztec empire once stood. Though it's critically endangered and rarely found in the wild, this little salamander is beloved by many and also one of nature's quirkiest creatures. With its adorable baby face—the result of neoteny (juvenile features in an adult animal)—this watery creature retains its tadpolelike features well into adulthood. Imagine if dogs were puppies forever!

Aside from being trapped in the fountain of youth, these neotenic salamanders have the extraordinary ability to regenerate any portion of their body. From their tails, limbs, or even portions of their spinal cords, an axolotl's regenerative capability extends all the way to its brain, heart, and other organs. When a human severs a limb, the body reacts to the wound by covering it up with skin tissue. The body of an axolotl, by contrast, can transform its cells into stem cells, which are fully capable of regenerating skin, bones, entire limbs, and veins. This means the axolotl can regenerate the severed body part perfectly each and every time. Scientists have yet to find a limit on how often a single axolotl can regrow the same part of its body.

Although we humans may not have the insane ability to regrow our body parts, we can work toward a different kind of growth by cultivating what psychologist Carol Dweck calls a "growth" mind-set. According to Dweck, people tend to fall into one of two categories: those of us with a "fixed" mind-set and those with a "growth" mind-set. When we believe that our traits and abilities cannot change or are innately linked to having "natural" talent, we are viewing ourselves with a "fixed" mind-set. If we believe that our talents and skills are acquired through effort and persistence, we have a "growth" mind-set. Those with a growth mind-set tend to achieve more because they believe that intelligence can be acquired and they don't view mistakes or lack of knowledge as weaknesses but rather as learning opportunities.

The good news is that even if you have a fixed mind-set, switching to a growth mind-set is as simple as wanting to change. Trying to adopt a new skill or habit is always daunting until you begin breaking down its parts. Are you trying to wake up earlier each day? Approaching this goal with a fixed mind-set may cause you to come up with excuses like, "I'm just not a morning person, I'm going to feel miserable." But approaching this goal with a growth mind-set is not only less daunting, it's more realistic! Breaking down the process of waking up earlier might mean not only getting to bed at a reasonable time but also waking up to something that excites you, like a fancy new coffee brand or a new outfit. When you adopt a growth mind-set, you accept your weaknesses and attempt to train yourself around them, rather than accepting your weaknesses because you assume they can't be changed.

The axolotl embodies this growth mind-set in its daily life, wherein even a challenge like the loss of a limb is surmountable. For a taste of this in our own lives, we should embrace the mantra: "I'm not there . . . yet." A key part of adopting a growth mind-set is keeping sight of where you want to go, while acknowledging that even if you aren't there at this very moment, someday you will be. Sure, an axolotl's limb may be missing today, but it may grow back by tomorrow. It's simply not there *yet*. Without trying to get where you want to go, you don't even allow yourself the opportunity to actually succeed—and what's the fun in that?

Take it from the optimistic axolotl's approach to life:
There is always an opportunity to grow.

THE
SHRIMP

*There is more to this tiny
creature than meets the eye,
and there is so much that
we can learn from it.*

When you hear the word "shrimp," one of two images probably comes to mind:

1. The small, pink, curly sea animal that we see in stir-fry

2. That little kid who could barely run a mile in gym class (uh, *definitely* not me)

Some of us may be familiar with how shrimp clean fish and eat their old scales, but beyond that, shrimp aren't exactly a creature that many of us dwell upon.

Of the more than two thousand shrimp species living in the ocean, the mantis shrimp and the pistol shrimp are two of the most fascinating. Shrimp are close cousins of lobsters and crabs in the crustacean family, all of which have tough exoskeletons (much like their even more distant relatives, the insects). Keep this in mind if you ever happen to attend a zoological-themed trivia night.

With that being said, let's embark on a wonderfully violent journey: into the world of the small and not-so-shrimpy mantis and pistol shrimp.

The Mantis Shrimp

If the ocean had yearbook superlatives, the mantis shrimp would easily glide into the "Best Dressed" category. They are deceptively gorgeous creatures to behold, but behind the facade they can be brutally vicious. Mantis shrimp can come equipped with two types of limbs, and they both sound like props in a Quidditch match: spearers and smashers.

Extending from the arm of the "spearer" species of mantis shrimp is a barbed spear appendage, which it uses to swiftly pierce soft-bodied prey once it's within reach. But this is not the reason why the mantis shrimp is so renowned in the animal kingdom. That honor goes to the larger "smasher" species, whose dramatic smasher appendages resemble a blunt club at the end of their arms. When prey is near, the shrimp will strike at a speed of 800 microseconds—at this speed, the mantis shrimp is technically capable of striking its prey over 300 times in the amount of time it takes a human to blink an eye.

This shrimp's striking speed is just a fun fact compared to the real damage it can do as it smashes down its claw with a force of nearly 1,500 newtons (that's about 340 pounds of force upon impact). No other small creature on the ocean floor, including crabs, other shrimp, and marine worms, stands a chance. Pair the mantis shrimp's force with its incredible speed and you understand the multiple instances of mantis shrimp breaking through aquarium glass and escaping. This is why aquariums either house the shrimp in special units or simply return them to the wild.

With all this action generated by a creature that's around the size of your hand (four inches long), there is a lot of gnarly physics at play. Striking with such force and speed underwater causes a cavitation bubble[*] to appear between the water and the mantis shrimp's claw. The water in the bubble is boiling, owing to this intense pressure, and the shrimp's claw packs a mighty punch. Even if the prey survives the attack, it is likely to go into shock or die from exposure to the boiling hot water of the pressurized cavitation bubble—a mere side effect of this whole spectacle.

Defending champ of the world's fastest limb movement, the mantis shrimp isn't meant to be served on a dinner plate.

---

* This is a bubble that forms when an incredible amount of pressure is applied to a generally low-pressure liquid.

The Pistol Shrimp

Imagine being able to kill or stun prey with no physical contact. Called "sonic hunting," this almost magical method has been mastered by the pistol shrimp. With one claw comically larger than the other, the pistol has a mechanism in its larger claw that allows it to shoot bulletlike bubbles at nearly 60 miles per hour toward its prey. It can only affect creatures and objects within a range of a couple of millimeters, but that makes it a nuisance to keep in tanks or study up close.

True to its namesake, the sound that the pistol shrimp makes when it fires bubbles from its claw has earned it the distinction of being one of the loudest creatures on earth. Also known as a "snapping shrimp," it makes a noise that's been measured at 200 decibels underwater—for comparison, a gunshot on land measures at around 150 decibels. This noise is the result of the bulletlike bubble that the pistol shrimp "shoots." The incredibly high pressure under which the bubble is formed is what makes an intensely loud noise when it pops. Not only does the shrimp emit a deafening sound, but it also packs a heated punch! Similar to the mantis shrimp, when the pistol shrimp's bubble bullet bursts, it releases a flash of light called sonoluminescence. Sonoluminescence is an indication that besides an extremely loud noise, extremely high temperatures are being released from the bubble as well—temperatures so hot that their bubble snap is hotter than the surface of the sun: 8,400 degrees.

To further put the level of noise this shrimp emits into perspective, consider that during World War II the US Navy would seek out colonies of pistol shrimp and station their submarines nearby. The amount of noise made by these colonies was capable of interfering with sonar technology, helping to camouflage the Navy's submarines from anyone trying to spy on or intercept their messages.

Noise, heat, and speed: the pistol shrimp dominates the genre of sonic hunting.

Size Never Mattered

Now that shrimp have become utterly terrifying for us all, it's time to reexamine our use of the term "shrimp" as a playground taunt. No, this isn't about wanting shrimp to reclaim their name—it's about understanding how we humans equate size with impact.

Many of us inherently understand that the physical size of a creature or a person doesn't define their value, but we often fail to apply that logic to our own actions. Our shrimp friends may be small, but their actions can literally leave other creatures stunned, or worse.

When was the last time you heard yourself or someone around you say, "It's fine, it's just this once," whether the subject was breaking a diet, failing to recycle a can, or smoking that cigarette? Hearing or saying "just this once" is all it takes for weeks, or even months, of planning and work to come to a screeching halt. "Just this once" is a small statement that can set off giant waves of impact.

On the flip side, seemingly small actions taken toward helping a friend or stranger can influence their mood (even their habits!) for much longer than we may think. Buying a coffee, giving a hug, lending an ear to listen—these are not just "nice" things to do, but ways to make another human feel valued. And they're not all about being selfless! Research has repeatedly shown that being kind and generous toward others boosts our mood and general outlook as well.

*Cocktail shrimp or not, we've all heard that
we can impact the world around us.*

Take it from the fierce shrimp:
*your potential influence has nothing to do with
size and everything to do with intention.*

THE
PARASITE

*Nature's stealthiest,
most devious organisms
are found in nearly every
climate and landscape.*

There are a handful of rare, brain-altering parasites that infect humans (don't google the pork tapeworm before bed).

Defined as an organism that lives either in or on a host organism of another species, the parasite thrives by taking nutrients away from its host. Capable of altering the behavior and fully controlling the organs of their host (including their brain), parasites come in many forms: fish, viruses, insects, and even bacteria.

Toxoplasma gondii

With a name that is all too fitting for a mind-controlling organism, *toxoplasma gondii* is one of the most commonly found parasites in the world. Toxoplasma is a single-celled microorganism of the protozoa family, a relative of bacteria that is estimated to infect approximately one-third of all humans worldwide with toxoplasmosis.

Before you consider guzzling hand sanitizer, reconsider, because:

1. Drinking hand sanitizer is sorta fatal.
2. Toxoplasmosis is not harmful to those of us with normal immune systems (unless you are pregnant—it can harm unborn children). Typically, the parasite exists in humans with zero effects.

If you are a mouse, however, not only is it surprising that you are reading this book, but you are also likely to die a unique death at the hands of this common foe. Healthy mice naturally avoid and fear the smell of cat urine, but mice infected with toxoplasmosis are manipulated by the parasite into being mildly *attracted* to the scent. That's right, toxoplasma alters the fundamental brain function of helpless rodents. Because the infected mice no longer avoid areas where cats have urinated, they end up hanging out wherever cats are regularly roaming—and being an easy snack for hungry felines.

Toxoplasma's journey doesn't end there. Like all parasites, toxoplasma infects other organisms for the sole purpose of growth and reproduction. Toxoplasma targets mice specifically so that it can reach a cat's digestive system, where it can reproduce successfully and leave the cat via fecal matter.[*] Often mice will even eat the toxoplasma-infected cat poop (ew), and so the parasitic cycle continues.

Here's to hoping every mouse your feline friend encounters continues to be afraid of them, because sometimes fear can be a healthy thing.

The Horsehair Worm

Looking a bit like the drain in your tub after your friend with long hair has taken a bath, the horsehair worm (*Paragordius varius*) is a thin, tangly creature that's anywhere from five to eleven inches in length. It's found in the waters of North and South America and is completely harmless to mammals. What makes this parasite truly disturbing, however, is its mind control over insects.

Living underwater, mature female worms will lay nearly 15 million eggs on solid surfaces like sticks or rocks. As the eggs

---

[*] *Unborn babies, who don't have fully developed immune systems yet, are susceptible to major complications brought on by toxoplasmosis if their mothers get infected. So pregnant peeps, avoid that kitty litter and consider training your cat to use a human toilet—it's possible, I think.*

Releasing large amounts of neurotransmitters inside its host, the horsehair worm can interfere with the signals created by the host's brain and assume absolute control over the creature.

hatch, horsehair larvae are born into the water and then survive if they are eaten by their first host. This first host is typically a mosquito larva looking for an easy snack. The parasite will latch onto the inside of its host and remain there as a cyst up until the mosquito matures enough to finally fly around and leave the water. Now flying around with the parasitic cyst inside it, the mosquito is likely to fall prey to a larger insect, such as a cricket, grasshopper, or beetle. In today's episode, the protagonist will be the chirpy cricket.

The horsehair worm larva has an impressive ability to sense when its intermediate host (the mosquito) has been eaten by a definitive host (the cricket). Once the cricket has eaten the mosquito, the worm larva will exit the mosquito, enter the cricket's stomach, and then exit it and live right in between its stomach and exoskeleton. That's right, this parasitic sucker makes a home for itself in between the cricket's organ and its outer body. Now situated in its new home, the parasite begins growing into its long, wormlike final form, which can reach up to a foot long. Here is where things get bizarre. While the worm absorbs nutrients from the cricket, it also begins manipulating its host's brain chemistry. Releasing large amounts of neurotransmitters inside its host, the horsehair worm can interfere with the signals created by the host's brain and assume absolute control over the creature.

Crickets cannot swim and will avoid water to prevent being drowned or eaten by a fish. However, crickets infected with the horsehair worm cannot seem to resist water and will leap straight in without hesitation, drowning in the process.

The horsehair worm has altered the cricket's brain chemistry so that the helpless creature is more attracted to bright light; as a result, it is tempted to walk right into the reflective surface of a body of water. When the horsehair worm senses that its host is submerged in water, it pierces through the cricket's body and escapes into the water, mature and ready to restart the life cycle.

But before your brain goes into macabre mode, it's okay, the cricket or whoever the horsehair worm decides to infest doesn't always die! Once the worm escapes its host, there's a slim chance that the cricket will make it back to shore and escape the watery H2O hell that almost ended it all. It'll continue living its life and may even mate and lay eggs like any other healthy version of itself. Most likely, though, the cricket will succumb to a watery death.

The horsehair worm: nature's literal buzzkill.

Toxicity

Parasites come in all shapes and sizes, from microscopic to bird-sized. No matter what they look like, a parasite's only goal is to steal energy, nutrients, and valuable resources from other creatures. There are a handful of rare, brain-altering parasites that infect humans (don't google the pork tapeworm before bed), but most of us will never have to be treated for them. This doesn't mean, however, that many of us aren't dealing with hidden toxic parasites of a different kind in our day-to-day life.

THAT PERSON who never seems to want to hang out unless they need something?

THE COWORKER who always sees the glass as half-empty?

THAT FRIEND you always find yourself in competition with and feel on edge around?

Alert: these are all examples of parasitic relationships! Sure, no one's growing inside of you and absorbing your nutrients, but that doesn't mean these people are not negatively impacting your life.

A positive relationship should make you feel cared for and safe, whether it's with a romantic partner, a family member, or even an employer. Other than making you feel unsafe, there are other, sneakier ways that a relationship with a toxic person can affect you. Is it truly a parasitic relationship? Let's discuss:

Do you feel worse about yourself after spending time with this person?

Just like an invasive parasite giving you physical symptoms, feeling worse after seeing a "friend" or a person you're dating is a bright red flag. But before you begin swearing off every single person who has ever made you feel down, pause. Being criticized occasionally or made the butt of a friend's bad joke isn't necessarily cause for ending a friendship. Toxicity has come into play when you find yourself feeling upset after *most* interactions with this person. If you find yourself consistently defending someone's negative actions toward you, it might be time to reevaluate your relationship with this person. Friends and romantic partners should make you feel good! If that's not the case, move on.

Do you constantly worry about whether your decisions will please this person?

Worried that your friend will criticize the restaurant you picked for dinner? How about your outfit? Will this person make fun of it? Will they roll their eyes if you tell them about that great article you read? It's okay, you think, I'll just smile and go along with it. This person means well, right?

Wrong.

It's one thing for a person to question you in a supportive way, but if they are regularly making you second-guess yourself to feel superior? Yeah, that's not cool. Your tastes, interests, and choices make up your personality. A person who judges your personality at every turn is truly too parasitic a person to have in your life.

Is your friend the Gossip?

Do you have that one friend who will without fail let you know that someone else's relationship is in shambles? How about the person who immediately starts badmouthing someone else once they're out of earshot? It's your friend, the Gossip.

The thing about the Gossip is that no one is immune. While it's a guilty pleasure to get the tea about someone else, don't for a second think you're not being talked about once

A positive relationship should make you feel cared for and safe, whether it's with a romantic partner, a family member, or even an employer.

you're gone. Breaking confidentiality is the ultimate indicator of not being trustworthy, and when you can't trust a friend, precious resources like time and energy become commodities.

The Parasitic Relationship: Is There a Cure?

The good news is that there is usually a way to remedy this situation. Start with an open and honest conversation, keeping in mind that you are trying to improve the relationship, not scrap it. But I'm not saying this will be easy. Either you and this person will resolve the issues at hand and work toward a healthier relationship, or you will agree to disagree and find yourself ending a toxic friendship. The latter scenario isn't ideal, but if you downplay the way someone or something makes you feel, the outcome will be even worse.

Take it from the shifty parasite:
if you feel exhausted or controlled by something or someone, they're probably taking up your precious resources and it's time to throw out the toxicity.

THE
WOMBAT

*Native to Australia, the wombat
looks like a larger, healthier
version of a guinea pig.*

Cousins of the koala, wombats are marsupials and carry their young around in pouches for six to seven months after giving birth. Scientists have only recently figured out something that has had them stumped for decades: what it is that these adorable and somewhat plain-looking creatures leave behind.

The Riddle of Wombat Poop

Pooping: there's an emoji based off it, we train our pets and children to do it properly, and there's even a $2 billion toilet paper industry literally banking on the fact that we poop.

That being said, the obsession with wombat poop among scientists is warranted. After all, the wombat is the only creature on earth that has been discovered to have cube-shaped droppings. Yes, you read that right: cube-shaped. As in dice, a Rubik's cube, whiskey stones. These are all items that resemble wombat poop.

So how exactly do wombats release these little cubes of joy that had scientists puzzled until 2018? It was originally hypothesized that the wombat's "exit hole" itself was cube-shaped. However, upon, uh, closer inspection, that was deemed to be untrue.

The mystery caught the attention of a group of physicists in North America, who had wombat roadkill shipped to them from Australia (imagine opening that package). Once they dissected the carcasses, scientists inflated the intestines of the wombat to observe its true shape. While the intestine of a human or a pig tends to have a smooth, rounded, and uniform shape when inflated, the wombat's intestine when inflated is

"Everything around you that you call life was made up by people that were no smarter than you."

—STEVE JOBS

irregularly shaped and has distinct indentations—imagine a pillow that has been compressed into something other than a pillow shape over time.

Because the walls of a wombat's intestine aren't a uniform shape, there isn't a uniform amount of pressure being applied when its poop is making its journey through the intestine. The wombat has cube-shaped scat, these scientists discovered, because this irregular pressure causes the feces to form sharp angles while in the intestine. Scientists still haven't entirely figured out what benefit there is to having cube-shaped poop, but one of the prevailing theories is that it makes the wombat better able to mark territory, since square poop doesn't roll around as much as round poop. We know two things to be true in nature: all living things have the capacity to reproduce, and all living things poop (except the demodex mite, but that's a whole other story). Wombat poop itself isn't special, but what makes it notable is how it transforms our everyday perception of what poop should look like. But quite frankly, it's still sh*t. Just because it's unique sh*t doesn't magically make it *not* sh*t.

Same goes for ideas. We may often hear that "brilliant minds" change the world with one idea, or that some people are just "born creative." Not only is this assumption debilitating, but it's simply untrue! Research has shown us over and over again that creativity is developed over time and it's not unique to certain individuals. This isn't to say that talent doesn't vary from person to person, but just like any ability, talent must be developed and nurtured to amount to anything. Our creative urges and output are the result of our experiences and environments—not some mysterious force exclusive to certain humans.

In today's world of social media clout, it's easy to mistake someone or something that receives a lot of attention as truly revolutionary. There's a lot of noise out there. Don't let it discourage or distract you from creating and trying. If you find yourself feeling like you're "not talented enough" or "not interesting enough" to start that fashion blog or to harness that business idea, remember that the point is not to constantly compare yourself to others. We are all innately creative. The trick is to give yourself the permission to create in your own way.

Steve Jobs was known to have said, "Life can be much broader once you discover one simple fact and that is everything around you that you call life was made up by people that were no smarter than you."

Take it from the endearing wombat:
We can all create sh*t. What makes your sh*t remarkable is how your ideas can shape it.

THE
SLOTH

Sloths are mainly known for being the slowest mammal in the animal kingdom.

When we talk about the sloth, it's usually in the context of laziness, or as a creative alternative to calling someone a turtle.

Sloths move an average of 123 feet per day. That's about 6 feet per minute. For comparison, humans walk an average of 270 feet per minute—45 times faster than our dear sloth buddy. These numbers don't make the sloth look so great, but if we look past the pace of his life and take a closer look at his lifestyle, we'll see that there is much more to this sluggish animal. Evolution has allowed the sloth to roam the earth (ever so slowly) for approximately 64 million years in a way that ensures the longevity of its resources.

With the lowest metabolic rate of any animal—it takes a sloth up to a month or more to fully digest its food—sloths can purposefully lower their metabolism in order to swim better. This allows them to hold their breath for up to 40 minutes underwater when needed. The sloth's slow pace also enables it to act as a living ecosystem[*] for local organisms such as fungus, mites, moths, and even a species of algae that successfully camouflages the sloth—protecting it from predators.

Though your device never performs as impressively in battery saver mode as it does when its screen is at full brightness, sometimes dialing it down is essential to conserve your resources. While it's awesome that you can fire on all pistons at all times during the day, it's only a matter of time until your fuel runs out. Sloths are slow because they have to be, but for us humans it's not that simple. In our world, there's a stigma

---

[*] *Scientists have counted over nine hundred different species living in the fur of a single sloth.*

Give yourself permission to zone out—without your phone.

attached to asking for days off or refusing an invitation to go out. Our Instagram feeds may claim that "self-care" consists of indulging in long naps and face masks, but reaping the benefits of a true battery-saving session requires more than such short-term solutions can deliver. Here are two ways to take it slow and truly save up your precious battery life.

Meditate

Meditating is great because it forces you to focus on something other than the plethora of thoughts that are probably zipping through your brain right now. Meditation doesn't have to be the corny, New Age-y experience that many influencers and "gurus" make it out to be. Simply sitting for 10 minutes on your bed or in a place that you find calming can allow you to reap the benefits of meditation.

To begin meditating, find a sitting position, either on a chair or the floor, that you're truly comfortable in. Don't worry about details like where your hands go—it's not a photo shoot. The point is just to feel at ease. Set a timer for 10 minutes and begin focusing solely on your breathing, with your eyes either closed or open. Again, finding whatever is comfortable for you and puts you at ease is the point here.

Challenge yourself to keep this up by meditating for 10 minutes a day for seven days. By the end of your first week, you may already begin to feel a difference. Over the long term, not only does a meditation practice improve your focus, but it prioritizes the conservation of your body's mental energy— taking a page straight out of the sloth's book.

Rein in Your Screen Addiction

Ten minutes doesn't seem like a long time—until we are forced to stay off our phones for that period. Try it: set a timer on your phone for 10 minutes and put it in another room. Chances are that you'll begin feeling an annoying sense of anxiety, or FOMO, within the first three minutes.

While our devices are fantastic at keeping us connected, there is such a thing as being *overly* connected. We may think we're "relaxing" before bed by mindlessly browsing the internet, but this habit is really just putting our brain into overdrive right when we should be winding down, and it can lead to major sleep issues, and possibly even anxiety issues, over time.

Give yourself permission to zone out—without your phone. Take it slow and don't respond immediately to texts or emails. Have a weird internet question and feel like you need to search for the answer like right now? It can wait. Write it down on a piece of paper. Feeling restless and just need something to do? Take a walk, which is also one of the best things you can do for your brain when you feel anxious.

Take it from the misunderstood sloth:
Taking it slow isn't a weakness, especially when your longevity depends on it.

THE
OYSTER

Great mother of pearl!

An oyster's main claim to fame may be the milky gems they produce, but this underwater creature does much more for the ecosystem by filtering up to 1.3 gallons of water per hour, helping to keep the ocean clean.

Pearls have earned a reputation for luxury dating back thousands of years, with mentions in ancient Hindu texts of gods adorned with the precious gem. In modern history, pearls have been embroidered into elegant gowns and have even adorned the necks and crowns of royalty.

The biology of pearl formation, while not known for being particularly luxurious, is elegant in its own right. First let's clear away a couple of common misconceptions around the formation of the pearl:

1. OYSTERS are not the only creatures that produce pearls. All shelled mollusks, such as conches, clams, mussels, and abalone, are capable of producing pearls. However, humans have considered the pearls they make far less valuable than the oyster's natural pearl.
2. PEARLS are not formed by a grain of sand infiltrating an oyster.

Let's expand upon number two. An oyster may begin forming a pearl in the presence of a grain of sand, but not because of the sand itself. A pearl begins to form when a portion of an oyster's mantle is damaged. The mantle is the part of the oyster that surrounds its organs: opening an oyster, you can see the mantle close to the edge, lining the shell.

When in doubt
do as the oyster does:
keep on swimming.

A pearl begins forming as an immune response inside the oyster. Anything from an external attack to a parasite to any organic matter can damage the mantle and trigger the creation of a pearl; this response is similar to our faces developing acne as a reaction to bacteria or oil, or white blood cells rushing to the site of a foreign body. Once the oyster senses that damage has occurred to its mantle, it begins secreting a combination of aragonite and conchiolin known as nacre or, more commonly, mother of pearl.

Layering like a gobstopper, the oyster covers its injury or parasite with a layer of nacre, followed by another layer, followed by another layer, followed by another layer, followed by a . . . you get the idea. It continues coating this area until a small mass develops and the damage has been completely contained. This process goes on for years, until a human discovers the oyster, peeks inside, and sees a small ball of nacre, aka a pearl, that has covered the oyster's injury.

Oysters show us how pain or difficulty can be used to create something beautiful. Experiencing a difficult life situation, such as the loss of a loved one or a health scare, may make us want to recede, but it's important to take time to understand what it means for the future.

Psychologists have found that when we experience adversity, it allows us to develop crucial coping strategies that can help us to handle setbacks better than people who have never experienced adverse events.

Now, there are obviously limits to how many setbacks a person can experience before losing the ability to see the "bright side." Just as a deadly parasite will result, not in a pearl, but in a dead oyster, there is no ideal number of setbacks we can experience before suffering permanent damage. So when in doubt, do as the oyster does: keep on swimming.

A real-life pearl of wisdom from the oyster:
Beauty is often born out of adversity.

THE
BIRD

It's a bird! It's a plane!
It's a . . . oh yep, it was a bird.

With approximately 18,000 different species of bird in the world, you're more likely to see a bird than a plane. Birds are among the first creatures we feel a sense of familiarity with as children: they have feathers, most of them can fly, and they have beaks. We see them singing outdoors, kept as colorful pets, and occasionally appearing on our dinner plates. From penguin to parrot, there are incredible and often nuanced differences between the bird species.

Ravens

No, not the ones from Baltimore—we're talking about Edgar Allan Poe's avian muse. Known to be clever and highly social, ravens are savvy enough to have inspired J. K. Rowling herself to name a Hogwarts house after them. (In the Harry Potter universe, Ravenclaws are known to be intelligent, creative, and clever, just like their namesake.*)

Ravens are opportunistic feeders in the wild, which means they have a flexible diet and will snack on whatever viable options are around. If they spot a small rodent, it can become a meal just as easily as some berries or fruit from a tree. Ravens often find food and hide it in surrounding areas so they can eat it later. It's hardly surprising that they've even been known to fly extra far away just to ensure a perfectly secure hiding spot for their food considering that ravens are also known to steal the hidden food of other ravens.

In fact, ravens not only keep tabs on other ravens so that

* Not a shameless plug for any specific Hogwarts house. Numerous online quizzes have told me I am a Hufflepuff.

they can steal their valuable treats; they also trick other ravens by creating fake hiding places for their food. Having decoy food spots works for them in part because ravens have fantastic memories and can easily relocate their hiding places.

When it comes to socialization, ravens do not live with other ravens in large flocks, as flamingos or geese do. Rather, these very territorial birds are combative toward other birds that may challenge them for the resources available on their claimed territory, especially when their eggs are involved.

Surprisingly, ravens do occasionally collaborate with other wildlife. Two examples involve wolves and lizards.

Ravens and Wolves

Upon reintroducing wolves to Yellowstone National Park in the 1990s, researchers observed that ravens would eat up to one-third of a wolf's kill. However, rather than attacking ravens or trying to hide from them, wolves were observed working with these conniving birds. Ravens were also observed calling out when they saw an injured or weak animal and leading wolves to it.

Why would ravens help the wolves? So they could benefit, of course! Not only do ravens lead wolves to their next kill, but they lead them to already dead animals so that the wolves can break open the bones and flesh, since ravens don't have the power to do that with just their beaks. Helping the wolf for the raven's own benefit makes sense, but what makes this phenomenon even more astounding is that ravens also lead other ravens to larger meals, such as an elk carcass, so that everyone can feed.

This alliance may seem like peculiar behavior given that ravens rarely help their fellow ravens (remember the whole stealing each other's food thing?), but it allows the birds to rely on one another when food is scarce.

Ravens and Uromastyx aegyptia

No, that's not a typo: the Uromastyx aegyptia, commonly known as the Egyptian mastigure, is a lizard found in the dry Arava Valley of Israel. The brown-necked raven, which lives alongside the Egyptian mastigure, has demonstrated a hunting behavior that is more commonly found in falcons: cooperative hunting. This hunting behavior has a higher rate of success than hunting solo, and the brown-necked raven has learned to take full advantage of it.

When the lizard is out of its burrow and exploring the world around it, unaware that its last few moments are approaching, the ravens take notice. At high speeds, two ravens will fly down and block the entrance of the lizard's burrow, cutting off its means of escape underground to safety. The rest of the ravens then swoop down and peck the exposed lizard to death—resulting in a midday meal for the flock.

This method of hunting among ravens has only recently been observed in two particular areas in the Arava Valley, leading scientists to believe that the birds are either learning from one another or a select number of adults have been teaching their young how to hunt cooperatively. Either way, the Egyptian mastigure are facing a challenge that never confronted their ancestors.

The Lance-Tailed Manakin

The world's most literal wingman is the male lance-tailed manakin found in tropical Central and South America. These birds are one of the few species in the animal kingdom that use a rare reproductive strategy called cooperative courtship: males of a species working together to convince a female that one of them is worthy of being her mate. If this reminds you of a Friday night out with friends, you're correct.

The male manakins, one alpha and one beta, engage in a courtship dance in which the two birds flit up and down and over one another in a leapfrog-esque motion to try to attract a female. Eventually, the less dominant male flies away, leaving the alpha male to continue the dance and wait for the female to invite him toward her.

The remarkable thing about male manakins' cooperative courtship behavior is that the two birds remain a team for multiple years as they take on different mates. So why do they tag-team a courtship dance?

There are two prevailing theories:

1. A group of male birds is louder than a single bird, making it easier to catch a female's attention.
2. Helping the alpha find a mate increases a beta's chances of finding a mate in the near future.

Cooperative courtship isn't for everyone, but it goes to show that having a good friend takes you a long way.

We're All in This Together

Let's get back to basics: ravens display cooperative behavior when the going gets tough, and manakins partner up to find a partner. Both species of bird choose to involve others in the pursuit of their goal knowing that cooperative behavior not only takes less energy but makes sense in the long run.

In today's culture, where we're inundated with messages about the "hustle" and being "self-made," we often overlook just how broad and, quite frankly, misleading these terms are. Both words imply that there's only one person working toward a goal. In reality, the most successful entrepreneurs, leaders, and creatives are all products of the advice and guidance they have received and, more importantly, the advice they have sought out.

Cooperation, whether between birds or humans, means asking for help when you need it and offering help when you're asked for it by others. Asking for help doesn't make you weak. In fact, it makes you stronger and leads you toward your end goals. It's important to nurture relationships and seek out mentors who can move you closer to your goals. In the workplace especially, it's important to find coworkers you can trust and go to for help. Knowing how to ask for help can make or break you at work—especially if you're looking to advance into a leadership position.

Whether it's getting set up on a blind date or wondering how to land that promotion, the first step in achieving your goal is acknowledging that you may need help and knowing that there's nothing abnormal about it. As one of the most social animals in the natural world, the human species has been built on teamwork: working together for one another.

Take it from the resourceful bird:

We must flock together in order to succeed.

THE ELEPHANT

*Besides being the largest
land mammals on the planet,
elephants would be wildly
successful at running for office.*

And no, not because they're gifted at raising campaign money (eleFUNDS anyone?). Elephants can teach us a remarkable thing or two about leadership.

Every elephant family is led by a matriarch, who isn't chosen based on a battle or on lineage. She is appointed because she has earned the respect of the rest of the elephants in the family.

But what does respect mean exactly for elephants? They bestow respect on the member of their herd that has made wise decisions time and time again—whether she has been the one to babysit the most youth or has a knack for choosing only the best, Michelin-rated spots for her family to eat.

In the human realm, leaders often gain their position by being the most vocal or receiving the most votes. Elephants, unlike humans, don't view leadership as a way to wield power; instead, they see a leader as a carrier of a family's compassion, trust, and long-term goals.

The matriarch shapes the everyday functions of the family, such as deciding which tactics and skills are to be taught to the baby elephants, thus shaping the future of her family. Even day-to-day functions such as feeding are heavily based on trust. If another elephant doesn't agree with the matriarch on where to eat, then it temporarily parts ways and then finds its way back to her. Sounds harmless, but over time parting ways too often makes you a vulnerable slab of prey, or worse: it could separate you from your family.

The matriarchs of elephant families earned their position by displaying wisdom gained from experience, the ability to prioritize the group's needs above anything else, and a pure lack of ego.

Take it from the sweet elephant:
True leadership is earned, not awarded.

THE
WOOD FROG

*For a creature with such
a bland name, the wood frog
is anything but.*

Nature's cryogenic experiment gone right, this amphibian has captured the attention of scientists for debunking much of what was believed about frog behavior during the winter season.

The wood frog can be found in woodlands all across Canada and north into Alaska; they are the only frogs known to live north of the Arctic Circle. As amphibians, all frogs are cold-blooded—meaning they cannot produce their own body heat. Instead, they adopt the temperature of the air or water around them. So how do they survive the cold without freezing to death?

Most frogs spend winter either underwater or underground. Due to the thermodynamic properties of a body of water the surface of a pond or lake is always colder than its bottom. So frogs and other amphibians can make a safe bet by hanging out at the bottom of their pond during wintertime. Frogs that go underground either take a mammal's former burrow or dig one and encase themselves there with mud. These frogs are more likely to be hunted by predators since they have to stay slightly exposed to air to avoid suffocating from being fully immersed underground.

So what about the wood frog? The only frogs known to exist so far north must have a trick up their amphibian sleeves in order to survive the winter. Brace yourself: the wood frog freezes to death in the winter and then, when springtime rolls around, springs back to life.

If you stumbled upon a frozen wood frog in the wild, you would probably think it's either a rock or a clod of cold dirt.

The frog is hard, cold to the touch, and completely unresponsive until it thaws for a few minutes—then its eyes open, its heart starts beating, and its breathing is jump-started. This zombie frog is anything but, even with its heart stopped. Its body is 70 percent frozen during the winter, with select organs completely safeguarded by cells surrounded by urea and glucose. Scientists are still unsure how exactly the frog's heart "comes back to life," but they remain hopeful that a way can be found someday to revive human tissue in the same way.

How exactly does the wood frog benefit from freezing rather than hibernating in the standard underwater way like other frogs? Freezing gives wood frogs a head start on reproduction since they thaw before most of the ponds, lakes, and rivers in their habitat, where other amphibians are hibernating within. Being active before other frogs enables wood frogs to breed with no competition for resources! They also can lay their eggs in vernal pools—seasonal pools of water created by melting ponds and bodies of water that dry up as spring and summer progress. The wood frog's eggs are safe from being eaten in vernal pools because they usually have no fish living in them. The early thaw catches, if not the worm, then the ultimate breeding ground.

For wood frogs, literally freezing their work functions during their resting time gives them an insane advantage when it's time to get back into the groove of everyday life. In 2017, 66 percent of Americans reported working while on vacation—and yes, checking your work email "just for a sec" counts as working. Many of us don't stop working when we're off the clock, even though the result is often burnout, fatigue, and intense psychological strain.

What exactly causes us to work on the weekends, or worse, during a vacation? The obvious answer is stress; the not-so-obvious answer is poor planning. The wood frog finds a secluded place in which to freeze before it settles in for the winter. We humans don't seclude ourselves from our jobs nearly as well. It's as easy as:

TURNING OFF WORK NOTIFICATIONS ON YOUR PHONE: Having a sense of FOMO is perfectly reasonable when you first turn off those phone notifications. To calm your nerves, remember: there will never be a work emergency that you'll discover via email or chat-app. Anything truly urgent is likely to warrant a phone call or at the very least a text message. Set your default away messages and be on your way to finally give your body and brain a needed rest.

MANAGING EXPECTATIONS BEFORE LEAVING: Even without FOMO, you may have convinced yourself that checking a notification here or there is harmless and may make you look "more reliable" to your office. Here's the fact: if you tell your office you won't be available but then continue responding to messages, you're setting unrealistic expectations for the rest of your tenure at that job. Not only that, what's the point of physically leaving the office if you never leave mentally? Manage expectations with your team and come to terms with the idea that nothing will fall apart just because you are not around.

Chilling Out

The survival advantage gained by the wood frog just by chilling out isn't all that crazy when we remember that, in the human world, not taking advantage of your vacation days makes you susceptible to burnout, lessens your chances of promotion, and even increases your odds for developing heart disease. Not only that, but your personal relationships will thrive the better you learn how to truly press Pause.

Take it from the cool wood frog:
*You can get ahead by learning how and when to
let yourself chill out.*

THE
OCTOPUS

First things first, let's dive into what the true plural form of octopus is:

O-C-T-O-P-U-S-E-S

Without getting into the grammar details of the ancient Greek versus ancient Latin roots of the word "octopus," just take my word for it and revel in the fact that you now know this cool, albeit jarring, very true fact.

There are over three hundred species of octopus, from some that are only a few inches long to others that grow to nearly 30 feet. We'll be focusing on the mimic octopus, which may be one of the most elusive characters in the world since Carmen Sandiego. Commonly known as the "chameleons of the sea," all octopus species can dramatically change the texture and color of their skin. The mimic octopus goes above and beyond that by impersonating other sea creatures' movements and behaviors.

The mimic octopus has been observed mirroring approximately fifteen other species, from snakes to various species of fish. It can shape-shift so well that it fools not only its predators but also its prey.

Here is a sampling of some of the animals that the mimic octopus is able to take after:

SEA SNAKE: The mimic octopus imitates the venomous sea snake by adopting its iconic black-and-white stripe pattern, burrowing itself into the seafloor, and then leaving out two of its arms and moving them around to look like one long sea snake.

LIONFISH: There is no specific reason why this fish is named after the lion. The two prevailing theories are that its wide, pointy fins resemble a fiery lion's mane, and that its venom can have quite ferocious effects. Either way, the mimic octopus impersonates this flamboyant fish by swimming in the open seas and crinkling and opening its legs wide. To the untrained eye, the octopus's patterning and movement would make it look exactly like a lone lionfish swimming happily along.

FLATFISH: Perhaps one of the mimic octopus's most iconic impersonations is of the flatfish, which is as flat as the ground itself and swims exclusively along the seafloor. Almost the same color as sand, the potentially poisonous flatfish fits right into the landscape. The mimic octopus can be seen folding itself into a similar shape as this fish and propelling itself along the seafloor just as a flatfish does. The mimic octopus changes not only its movement but its coloration to blend into the seafloor.

The animals that the mimic octopus often imitates have one thing in common: they're mostly poisonous or pose some other sort of advantage over the octopus's own natural defenses. By mimicking animals that are less likely to be attacked, octopuses protect themselves from predators that would normally see them as a tasty afternoon snack. In other words, "Fake it till you make it."

From impostor syndrome[*] to low confidence, we've all been in situations where we could have used a pep talk or

---

* Impostor syndrome is the psychological pattern of doubting the validity of your accomplishments and consistently feeling like a fraud.

maybe even "liquid courage" to lift our spirits. But these boosts are temporary. What do we do before other big life moments? Before that big presentation, before saying hello to that one person, or even before starting on a major assignment, it pays off to fake it till we make it.

Like most things, that's easier said than done. Here are two simple ways to adopt this mind-set.

Guess What? Everyone Else Is Faking It Too

It can sometimes feel like everyone around you is the epitome of confidence. But once you begin to open up about your own insecurities, you might begin to get a different picture. From your coworker who always seems to know what to say to that one friend who never seems to get nervous at parties, and even celebrities! Everyone feels self-conscious at one point or another. James Corden, the comedian and Emmy Award–winning host of *The Late Late Show*, has publicly opened up and said, "I still might get fired. I think like that every day."

At some point, we just need to fake it till we make it. This doesn't mean be inauthentic. By addressing what you're not confident about, you'll be able to curate a more confident version of yourself just by *wanting* to improve. For instance, in writing this book, every time I sat down to talk about a critter I tried to envision myself hanging out with Steve Irwin in some cool forest, or accepting the Pulitzer Prize—not stuck at a desk feeling like I forgot English and eating a bowl of cereal.

So relax, you're not the only one.

Dress for the Role You Want

No, this does not mean it's okay to impersonate a police officer.

You know that feeling you get when you wear your favorite outfit? Imagine channeling that feel-good energy into whatever task is making you feel uneasy. I had a friend in high school who wore formal business attire when taking the SAT because she felt like the outfit made her more observant and poised. Did she do well? Absolutely. I wore the sweatpants I woke up in, but that's also what I felt most at ease and confident in. Did I get a good score? Let's ask Steve Irwin and the Pulitzer committee . . .

It may feel like it's "all in your head," but when you're feeling good, it's hard for that confidence not to translate into your actions. Dreading going to the gym? Wear an outfit that makes you feel like a gym rat. Pitching an idea to your team? Throw on that outfit that gives you entrepreneur vibes.

The outfit that makes you *feel* like you're playing the part can actually help you *land* that part. Again—preferably in a lawful manner.

The octopus disguises itself as different species to evade predators, and we can take a cue from this, faking it until we make it through a low self-confidence moment.

Take it from the versatile octopus:
faking it to make it can help you get to where you want to be.

THE
AVOCADO
TREE

*The avocado. The one green
thing most of us love to eat,
this fruit (yes, it's a fruit) has
somehow become the icon of
an entire generation.*

We see it everywhere—on toast, served up as guacamole, designed onto cell-phone covers, in our Instagram feeds, and in every salad imaginable. We can hardly imagine a world anymore in which the avocado isn't staring into our souls with its creamy interior and high nutrient content. The story of how we got the modern-day avo is one of survival, evolution, and sheer luck, because truth be told, about 12,000 years ago, our friendly neighborhood avocado should have gone extinct.

During the Pleistocene Era, aka the last Ice Age, which ended 11,700 years ago, a group of behemoths known as megafauna roamed the earth. They included *Megatherium*, the giant ground sloth that could weigh up to four tons, and *Glyptodon*, the giant armadillo that could grow to the size of a small car. During this era, in what is modern-day Central America, avocado trees thrived thanks to these giant animals.

In order to thrive, avocado trees need a way to spread their seed so that more trees can grow. The seed from a ripe avocado that has fallen from its tree won't grow into a healthy new avocado tree unless it's transported elsewhere, because an avocado tree needs a *lot* of sunlight to flourish. A seed planted near an existing tree will be literally overshadowed and receive minimal sunlight.

So how did avocado seeds get transported to open areas with lots of sun? The answer begins with the prehistoric giant sloth, and *Megatherium* poop. The prehistoric giant sloth ate avocado fruits whole and had no problem moving the seeds through its digestive system. As these giant sloths grazed, they'd make their, uh, deposits far from the original avocado tree—deposits that contained avocado seeds.

When the Pleistocene Era ended, however, most of these creatures went extinct. Without these large mammals to eat whole avocado fruit, there was no way for the avocado seed to be spread around widely enough for healthy new avocado trees to grow.

cue sad music

Thus, the end of the last Ice Age should have been the end of the avocado.

So how exactly did we get to a point where our society is currently consuming an average of 4 billion avocados per year? Who else has an awesome track record when it comes to meddling with nature? Humans!

Around the same time *Megatherium* was dying out, humans had begun toying with agriculture. Much like modern-day humans, our ancestors loved the smooth, fleshy interior of the fruit and decided to grow and farm it themselves! Suddenly, avocado seeds no longer needed to be transported to wide-open areas via large animals—they were being planted and cultivated by us.

Changing the avocado tree's environment initially put it at risk of extinction, but things took a turn for the better when humans turned its fate in a new direction. Known as a "ghost of evolution," the avocado tree is an anomaly of survival and evolution. Even without the benefit of the giant sloth's perfect digestive system, a new curated environment allowed the tree and its fruit to outlive the Ice Age.

Much like the avocado tree, you may or may not thrive depending on your environment. You may be surrounded by people who completely support your goals, or by people who

Caring for yourself means seeking out situations that motivate you toward the future you want for yourself.

don't even know you exist. Either way, these people can severely affect your mood and future. Caring for yourself means seeking out situations that motivate you toward the future you want for yourself. That could mean rethinking the people you choose to be around.

Have a fitness goal? It could be time to form a new group of friends who don't live off of fast food. Thinking about making a career shift? Finding a motivating environment may require something as major as moving to another city or as simple as surrounding yourself with professionals from the new industry. Either way, a change of any kind requires some sort of change of environment.

We've all experienced moments when simply changing clothes or walking out of a room shifted our mood. Imagine that happening on a larger, more impactful scale! Care for yourself by first acknowledging and then embracing a change in your environment.

Take it from the enticing avocado:
A change in environment can spell the difference between growth and extinction.

THE NIGHT-BLOOMING CEREUS

Roses are red, violets are blue.

Plants have a busy schedule,

Let me show you.

Flowers have evolved to follow the blooming routine that works best for them.

"Evolutionary sophistication" isn't what most of us think of when we describe plants. Humans have been around for approximately 200,000 years, but plants have had the head start on us of being on the planet for approximately 500 million years. In this time, they've learned to thrive on land, water, and even rock. Whether in the form of trees, shrubs, lily pads, or delicate flowers, plants define both natural and man-made landscapes.

Flowers are perhaps the most recognizable plant. Types of flowers vary, depending on where you live. In Holland the tulip reigns supreme, while the jasmine and marigold are central to the cultural and religious history of India. Colorful and fragrant, flowers have given humans a very organic way to show their feelings toward one another. There's more to blooming plants, however, than pretty petals.

Let's look at the tulip, jasmine, and marigold, flowers with vastly different behaviors. The tulip closes its petals at night, the jasmine blooms at night, and the marigold stays open at all times of the day. This is not a fluke! Through evolution, each flower has learned when is the best time of day for it to bloom.

The night-blooming cereus, a type of cactus flower that blooms only at night, is the perfect example of a species that has become specialized. Most cereus flowers open their petals only at nightfall; however, some species of cereus bloom only once a year. For the night-blooming cereus, the hawk moth and nectar-feeding bat are responsible for spreading its pollen. Since both of these creatures are active only at night, the cereus finds it advantageous to open and emit a fragrance only in the evening.

The tulip, on the other hand, closes its petals shut during the evening or on cloudy days. During the daytime, it opens its petals, ready for the sun and its many pollinators to pay it a visit. Because pollen is best transferred when dry, the tulip shuts its doors at the first sign of rain or when skies become dark or overcast to prevent its pollen from becoming wet or washing away.

Flowers have evolved to follow the blooming routine that works best for them. Sure, the cereus is missing out on sunlight, but it has adapted to not need it. The same is true of the tulip, which, like me, loves the rain but not to the point of having a bad hair (or pollen) day.

A routine is as beneficial to you as it is to flowers, helping you bloom into a better version of yourself. Having a routine doesn't require always waking up early or eating the same meal every day. Like all things, your routine can and should be flexible. The point of a good routine is to eliminate the stress of the little things and bring out your strengths. There's no shame in changing up your routine and fine-tuning it until it feels just right for achieving these benefits.

For a long time, setting a routine for myself felt "out of character," as if I was succumbing to pressure to adopt a lifestyle all about wake up–work–eat–run errands–eat–sleep and not much else. But creating rituals and moments when I can feel truly myself and designating days of the week when I do certain chores has allowed me to have more moments when I'm doing what I enjoy instead of just constantly catching up on errands. Rather than forcing yourself to stick to a schedule that doesn't make sense for you, create one that makes every day feel a little bit brighter.

Do you work better late at night? Create a routine that allows you to finish your errands before nightfall, making your nights stress-free. How about working out? Do you feel completely exhausted after work? Then don't try to work out after you get home, but instead carve out gym time for that point in the day when you tend to feel naturally more active.

Don't let the word "routine" scare you. Start small, like listening to your current favorite song at the same time each day, or calling your grandma* every Tuesday. As long as you start somewhere, you're on your way to creating a more robust routine over time!

Self-care is tied closely to routine because creating moments in your day that you truly look forward to is a win-win not only for yourself but for your creativity, your family, and your goals.

Take it from the reliable night-blooming cereus:
*Knowing what time of day works best for you
helps you truly bloom.*

IN CONCLUSION:

LOVE THY NATURE

True self-care starts with wanting to improve our lives. Some of this self-improvement comes naturally, and some of it feels like a real struggle. The truth is that we are all just built differently. Identifying our strengths and weaknesses, and challenging what we *think* is true about ourselves, is where it all begins.

Thank you for taking this journey with me. Whatever you decide to take away from this book—whether it's declaring the pistol shrimp your new life mascot or building a garden shrine to your avocado tree, be proud that you are giving yourself a chance to better understand your physical, emotional, and mental health. Maybe I've told you more than you wanted to know about parasites! But my hope is that by paying more

33 percent of amphibians, 50 percent of primates, and 68 percent of plants are at risk of extinction.

attention to the rhythms of nature and the curious creatures in the world around us, we can learn how to get back to basics with ourselves. Because the fact remains that we humans don't have all the answers, not even close. Taking a cue from the natural world can ground us all.

Health and well-being don't end or begin with us: these things extend to our outlook toward the Earth. A good number of the creatures mentioned in this book are currently on the endangered species list. And overall, nearly 33 percent of amphibians, 50 percent of primates, and 68 percent of plants are at risk of extinction. Human activity—acidification of the oceans, global warming, and deforestation—is to blame for our planet being at risk. We are all in this together, and self-care shouldn't be a solitary act. It should also include caring for the planet and her species. If we don't protect the Earth, our planet will suffer its own kind of burnout.

Much like self-improvement, helping the environment begins with awareness—awareness of the world around us. To that end, I leave you with a few simple ways to care for the planet and yourself:

Unplug and Unscrew

Unplug your devices when you're not using them. It turns out that electronic devices (TVs, toasters, laptops, etc.) still use electricity when they're plugged in and turned off! Unscrew those old-school incandescent lightbulbs and replace them with either LED or compact fluorescents. Energy-saving lightbulbs are better for the earth, and they save money because they last longer. According to the EPA, replacing just one incandescent lightbulb in every home in America would save enough energy to provide electricity to three million American homes. And be sure to recycle your old bulbs!

Cut Back on Meat

Roughly twenty-five times more energy is required to produce one calorie of beef than to produce one calorie of corn for human consumption. I won't go all vegetarian manifesto on you. But I will recommend that you start by foregoing meat just one day a week. The health and environmental benefits are outstanding. Double self-care!

Consume Meaningfully

The key to our planet's future is using less. Less fuel, less packaging, less waste. Shop at second-hand stores when you can, bring your own reusable bags to the grocery store, and buy grains and other foods in bulk when possible to help reduce your overall footprint. Plus, you'll be saving money to spend on all those self-care massages. Hellooooo, heated stone massage!

Nature and Nurture

Give yourself permission to become nature's best friend. Challenge yourself to change your habits, to see how less is more, and to find creative ways to reduce your carbon footprint. Yes, swearing off plastic straws and boycotting polluting industries sounds absolutely delightful, but remember, it's not the only way. There are so many ways to make an impact. Start small, and focus on change in your community rather than trying to save the world. We'd all be better off by focusing on what's close to home and going local.

Unlike a traditional safari, your self-care safari has a beginning but, hopefully, no end. Nurture yourself and practice self-care in every ecosystem you may encounter: at work, with friends and family, and especially the one you cultivate wherever it is that you call home.

Take it from our strange, marvelous, and inspiring planet:
Nurturing nature is self-care for us all.

ACKNOWLEDGMENTS

A book doesn't just take a village, it takes a world. An entire goddamn planet.

Starting at the beginning with my parents. Mummy, thank you for unconditionally loving me through every tantrum, annoying argument, and most of all, weird decision I have made—and oh *bhagavan* have I made some weird decisions. You put me in a storytelling class when I was eleven years old, you may not remember it but I sure do, largely because well . . . it worked. Thank you for being one of the first people who thought I was a good writer. That changed my life.

To my Dad, to whom I am forever grateful for subscribing to *Highlights* magazine and *Reader's Digest*. Those publications and our conversations shaped the way I consumed and shared information. For every *Planet Earth* episode that you *insisted* our family watch together—needless to say, that left an impression on what I value and how I view not only the planet, but how I define the meaning of family.

Rohan, on our very long flight to Southeast Asia you shared amazing facts about enough animals to write three more books. To say you got me excited about actually writing this thing is an understatement. Thank you for keeping me excited, grounded, and beyond all else, being someone who truly understands the magnificence of both squirrels and llamas.

The past year, staying motivated proved to be a struggle. Utsav, your enthusiasm, support, and just general excitement about life is what made this entire process so much fun. Whether it was "accidentally" telling everyone we'd meet that I was writing a book or squealing every time I finished a round of edits—you are the reason this book was actually finished on time. I am truly marrying up.

To my brilliant, fellow author sister-friend, Alisha. Thank you for being my guide on all things publishing world and sitting with me late at night listening to my incoherent rants about wood frogs. *All My Friends Are Planets* is a masterpiece and every child should have the privilege to read it.

All the wonderful people at Trello—thank you for allowing me to be a part of your team. Not only as a teammate, but as a productivity tool, my Trello board is how my book was born beginning to end. Leah, you casually mentioned I should write an article about animals while we stared at beehives. Not only are you one of the most creative people I've met, your voice is the one I hear as I edit my own writing. Thank you for shaping me into a better writer and person. Stella, the support and enthusiasm you offered at the beginning of this writing process is what gave me the confidence of, well, actually doing this thing. Thank you for your guidance and the resources you threw my way.

To Sean, thank you for . . . everything. For answering my relentless questions, for assuring me that this wasn't all one amazing fever dream, for being my advocate before I even knew I had one. Thank you for sharing your vision with me. You are my wonder woman.

To my editors, Jessica and Alivia. Never let anyone tell you that you aren't the most hardworking people on this planet. As much as I wanted to refute any new suggestions to my writing, you both were, simply, usually right. You both brought this vision to life, I am forever grateful to you both. Thank you for humbling me and, above all else, not killing me for not always meeting my deadlines.

Gemma, you are the most talented person on earth. Literally on the entire earth.

Having you involved in this project means everything to me and you somehow created art I could have only dreamt of. Please hang out with me when you're in New York.

To the wonderful people at *Nature*, National Geographic, and Wikipedia—these are resources that made this book factually accurate and this earth more comprehensible.

Thank you, *Brown Girl Magazine*, for being the first to ever publish my work and making me feel "real."

Thank you to all the readers of Fuss Class News for wildly inflating my ego and making me think I'm funny.

Shwetha, Ariha, Ritu, and Pooja Masi, thank you for being my cheerleaders, my sounding board, and truly, my role models.

Taylor, thank you for your text messages in ALL CAPS and your unreal design advice.

Evan, thank you for lending me your books as research. The octopus section also thanks you.

To the best groups of people in my world: Oochki, BFOAT, and Bison. I love you.

To Joe Bar in Seattle for giving me a space to begin my writing career.

Jeff Corwin, you were my inspiration growing up. I would not be at all bothered if you'd like me to cohost any new wildlife show you may have. Like not at all.